To: Stella, My Cuz + Best Friend!

From: Lydia, with much love!

Date: May 13, 2001

Happy Mothers Day!

The Two of Us

Ellen Small and Jim Dale

STARK BOOKS
an Andrews McMeel
Publishing Imprint

To the two of us at the Vineyard.

The Two of Us copyright © 2000 by Ellen Small and Jim Dale. All rights reserved.
Printed in China. No part of this book may be used or reproduced in any manner
whatsoever without written permission except in the case of reprints in the context of reviews.
For information, write Andrews McMeel Publishing, an Andrews McMeel Universal company,
4520 Main Street, Kansas City, Missouri 64111.

00 01 02 03 04 RDS 10 9 8 7 6 5 4 3 2 1

Small, Ellen.
     The two of us / Ellen Small and Jim Dale.
          p. cm.
     ISBN 0-7407-1088-5
     1. Women—Psychology—Miscellanea. 2. Female friendship—Miscellanea. 3. Female
friendship—Pictorial works. I. Dale, Jim. II. Title.
HQ1206 .S59 2000
302.3'4—dc21   00-34440

Book design by Holly Camerlinck

——————— Attention: Schools and Businesses ———————

Andrews McMeel books are available at quantity discounts with bulk purchase for educational,
business, or sales promotional use. For information, please write to: Special Sales Department,
Andrews McMeel Publishing, 4520 Main Street, Kansas City, Missouri 64111.

The two of us . . .

. . . feel like we've known each other forever.

The two of us . . .

. . . trust each other with secrets, like our real weight.

The two of us . . .

. . . would drink from each other's straws
but nobody else's.

The two of us . . .

. . . could order the other's exact meal in a restaurant, including the special instructions like "broiled, not fried . . . extra lemon . . . dressing on the side."

The two of us . . .

. . . can cook if we have to but can carry out even better.

The two of us . . .

. . . always want to lose seven pounds.

The two of us . . .

. . . have lost (and gained) the same seven pounds
over and over.

The two of us . . .

. . . despise petty gossip but appreciate social "news."

The two of us . . .

. . . hate chase scenes in movies because people
are just chasing each other but love love scenes
because the two stars finally get together
like they should've all along.

The two of us . . .

. . . could be Martha Stewart if we had more time
to make dried-leaf place mats and color-coded
spice jars.

The two of us . . .

. . . never get our cars washed.
What exactly is the point?

The two of us . . .

. . . are smarter than most men.

The two of us . . .

. . . don't go beer drinking.
We like umbrellas in our drinks.

The two of us . . .

. . . are trying hard not to be our mothers.

The two of us . . .

. . . would be lucky to turn out as well
as our mothers did.

The two of us . . .

. . . never get that "rush" from exercise.

The two of us . . .

. . . cry at TV commercials about reunions.

The two of us . . .

. . . can eat a party-size bag of M&M's in one sitting.

The two of us . . .

. . . are pretty skeptical when our kids swear
they'll feed the dog/cat/goldfish/hamster/gerbil.

The two of us . . .

. . . can never remember having a good haircut.

The two of us . . .

. . . have a built-in polygraph when it comes to knowing whether homework is done.

The two of us . . .

. . . both squint in the mirror and tilt our heads
the same way when we try on clothes.

The two of us . . .

. . . blame our figures on having children
(and hate women who have had children
and still have flat stomachs and who are
probably annoying in other ways, too).

The two of us . . .

. . . swear by the same diet:
the starve-yourself-until-the-weekend-when-you-
have-to-fit-into-that-tight-dress diet.

The two of us . . .

. . . think each other's children are perfect.

The two of us . . .

. . . sing along to old rock 'n' roll songs on the radio when we're alone in the car until somebody in the next car notices.

The two of us . . .

. . . could shop for black pants, black skirts, black dresses, black blazers (and pretty much any black clothing) forever.

The two of us . . .

. . . know exactly what we got on the SATs
but still have that same dream about forgetting
our locker combinations.

The two of us . . .

. . . have no tolerance for women who complain about
not being able to gain weight.

The two of us . . .

. . . know the name of the first boy we ever
1) kissed
2) French-kissed
3) did other stuff with.

The two of us . . .

. . . were totally opposed to plastic surgery
. . . until recently.

The two of us . . .

. . . think intelligence is sexy.

The two of us . . .

. . . don't have gray hair . . . anymore.

The two of us . . .

. . . put off taking our cars in for service until
they make really bad noises or something falls off.

The two of us . . .

. . . love dancing and,
until we find men who do too,
are going to keep dancing with each other.

The two of us . . .

. . . love to talk.

The two of us . . .

. . . know when to listen.

The two of us . . .

. . . know that if one of us likes a book,
the other one will, too.

The two of us . . .

. . . are going to organize our family photos . . . soon.

The two of us . . .

. . . are not "at one with nature."

The two of us . . .

. . . are a little bit crazy about our teeth.
(There's no such thing as too much flossing.)

The two of us . . .

. . . like to shop by catalog because you don't
have to try anything on in front of anybody,
especially the seventeen-year-old,
ninety-eight-pound salesgirl.

The two of us . . .

. . . can always spot a hairpiece.

The two of us . . .

. . . secretly look at guys' butts. (Okay, so it's obvious.)

The two of us . . .

. . . can calculate end-of-season discounts in our head but use the "around" method of balancing our checkbooks.

The two of us . . .

. . . can smell whether food is past its expiration date.

The two of us . . .

. . . don't clean behind refrigerators, freezers, washers, or dryers because there's a whole world back there we don't want to know about.

The two of us . . .

. . . promise to use our cell phones only for emergencies
. . . like checking our voice mail.

The two of us . . .

. . . have both perfected the art of antiseptically papering toilet seats in public bathrooms.

The two of us . . .

. . . would never tell anyone the other's age.

The two of us . . .

. . . went to natural childbirth classes and then begged for drugs.

The two of us . . .

. . . understand January White Sales but don't get March Madness.

The two of us . . .

. . . never forget each other's birthdays.

The two of us . . .

. . . call each other sometimes just to make sure everything's okay.

The two of us . . .

. . . worry about our parents.

The two of us . . .

. . . worry about our kids.

The two of us . . .

. . . worry too much.

The two of us . . .

. . . sometimes get annoyed with each other, but . . .

The two of us . . .

. . . can't stay mad at each other.

And . . .

. . . If there were one breath of air left on earth,
we'd split it.